MW01141352

Being
in the
Moment

poetry, photographs & drawings
by
dolores giustina fruiht

[signature: dolores giustina fruiht]

The Crucible

Published by
The Crucible
P.O. Box 823
Bodega Bay, CA 94923

Cataloging-in-Publications Data

Fruiht, Dolores G.
Being in the moment / by Dolores Giustina Fruiht
p. cm.
ISBN 0-9636493-3-7
1. Gift books. 2. Poetry, belle lettres. 3. Photography, artistic
I. Title
PS3556.R8548B4 1993   811.54
                                                       93-71546

Book production by Cypress House, Fort Bragg, CA

Manufactured in the United States of America

10 9 8 7 6 5 4 3 2 1

I dedicate this book, with love, to my grandchildren.
It is my hope they can always honor life's urgency of inner search.

"...I pluck you out of the crannies,
I hold you here, root and all,
Little flower — but if I could understand
What you are..."

Flower in the Crannied Wall
Alfred Lord Tennyson

Acknowledgments

So many people have contributed time and assistance to the evaluation of this book, and I wish to thank all of them, men and women, colleagues and friends.

I have benefited greatly from the encouragement and support, from editorial comments and proofreading, from all constructive and critical comments. It has been a true gift to explore emerging patterns and motivations in our lives with such integrity.

For years much of the manuscript was detained, motionless, waiting within her shell, searching for a way out, trying to "see." Words unlocked, provided images of my truth at the moment of writing. It matters not if they remain true, they gave me perspective to the unfolding cosmos to which we all belong. They revealed to me my need to accept, reflect, and move between universal opposites.

I wish to also acknowledge the influence and inspiration of the many books it has been my joy to read. Artists, historians, philosophers, sociologists, paleontologists, physicists, theologians, poets, dreamers and more. New and shifting paradigms expand and deepen our consciousness. To use Teilhard de Chardin's words, "incorporated knowledge is both a mirror and directive agency." To these scholars, women and men, living and deceased, who have helped me to honor and define my creative process, and to grow from it, I am ever grateful.

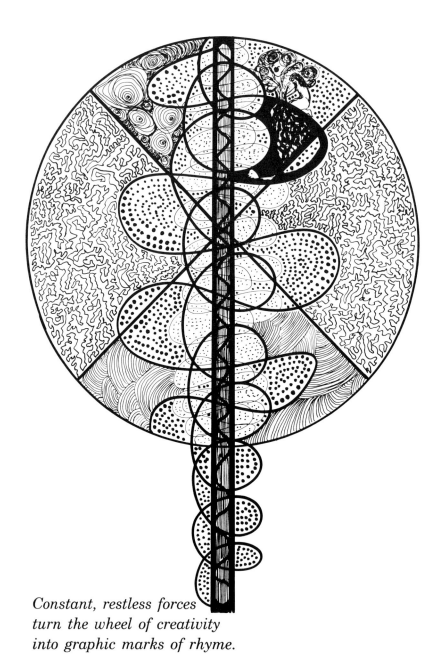

*Constant, restless forces
turn the wheel of creativity
into graphic marks of rhyme.*

Introduction

I love Dolores' work — the drawings, the photos, the poetry, the journal entries — all echo and subtly reflect on one another.

I am particularly moved by the dream images — the moving wall of black bodies; the transparent beating heart, chambers visible; the water, lapping and searching everywhere with its wet fingers.... There is a richness of real life in these pages, seen and felt and imagined again, and rendered into images that touch the mind and heart.

There is an acknowledgment of the traditions and conventions of formal art in these pages, but there is also a strong, un-self-conscious assertion of raw and original feeling. The life experience that births these fluid gems, (like tears), surges like the old Protestant hymn — "...wheat and tares together sown / into joy and sorrow grown."

The whole impact is like a service of hymns — the complex, universal pains and happinesses and uncertainties are distilled and turned into insights, simply and clearly rendered, like images in a memorial stained glass window suddenly illuminated from behind as the sun comes out from behind a cloud.

— Jeremy Taylor

Jeremy Taylor is a Unitarian Universalist minister who has been a dream worker and teacher of dream work for over 25 years. He teaches at Starr King Seminary and other Graduate Theological Union schools, and with Matthew Fox at the Institite in Creation Spirituality. He is the author of *Dream Work* and *When People Fly and Water Runs Uphill* .

Preface

This book invites you to share an inner process.

Like a tree, my branches stretch in many directions, sometimes full with rich foliage, and sometimes bare, fragile and vulnerable. Varied are the stages of any tree before maturity. Long and silent the clustering of seasonal fruit; transition to evolvement.

My branches own and even covet masks as they change with advancing seasons. Twigs bend and break in the shifting, sweeping wind. After all, who can allude to fear or threat with complete ease? We have all watched with envy as the snail withdraws into his spirally coiled shell for protection. And, does not our globe also enfold within its crusty surface her layers of substance? The seed is no sooner enclosed than it emerges. Forces dormant, awaken. The external and internal are connected. In my evolution, I contribute to the formation of that "greater pattern" as importantly and critically as any one or all. I am not unusual, unless it is unusual to recognize how usual one is.

About ten years ago, the whole world became a blur. Irregular lines began to form as restless currents churned within. With a slight adjustment of the mask, all disturbing oscillation seemed to still, for the moment. Cancer became a threat. Fear, a chilling fact. A successful marriage of thirty years soon disintegrated.

Body, mind and soul suffered and questioned. Liv-

ing became a vast ocean of opposing and undulating tides. My creative process was, is, a dolorous one. I am forever stilled with reverent wonder. Can or does creativity take form in any other manner?

Cancer became a truth. And I felt like a cork bobbing in a stormy, uncontrollable sea. No longer was my ego in charge, rather overwhelming forces dislodged it. My body felt very foreign, my mind unpredictable, but even in this despair a presence pervaded. Some unknown, yet known was pulling me.

At this moment, "upon this bank and shoal of time," my unbridled pen began to place in prose and verse form all the unformed. A budding branch was curving, arching, crossing, growing, becoming, a sacramental gift given to be discovered and to be shared. To express the innermost soul in any manner, be it movement in dance, sculpture, song or written word, demands an inexhaustible and contemplative study of human nature and her diversified patterns. This process is life-long. We have the freedom (and obligation) to give shape to the sapling.

The mystery of "self" will yield her hidden secret only as wo / man becomes conscious of the deeper roots of her being.

Come, wade into these surging waters, and feel the JOY of growth slowly drown the pain of fear. Observe mind's inmost core, mysteriously present everywhere, extend into streams of new consciousness, like deep-lying roots of an established tree. Be aware...that this *moment (the only moment there is) is only temporary, as life's movement is never ending and ever transforming.*

My first book, Becoming, *followed by* Silence, *afforded the receptacle out of which* Being *became. Yet the three are inseparably linked; a hallowed chain of unbroken unity, reality.*

And the cosmic wheel continues to turn....

Within heart's open chamber
flowers life's harmonic deed.

A DOLL

A doll just new,
Crisp, smooth, strong,
I was best of boxed toys
Nothing yet wrong.

I had eyes that shut,
Cheeks red and full
And a voice box too.
Marked "just pull."

Unsoiled as yet
By anxious hands,
I'd sit on the bed
Or perhaps just stand.

So proud they were
At the brightness of me,
So proud I was
None could foresee

That season, that fateful season,
I was caught, dropped in the rain.
Down streamed my hair,
My face became stained.

My leg had a twist
My heart had a break,
The hollow within
A throbbing ache.

No longer the doll
That stood so proud,
Dis-illusion was wrought
And wrought aloud.

As I squirmed in the box
Of toys faded and worn,
Silently sharing
And quite forlorn,

I felt from the sky
The sun's warm giving
"Knowledge of dying
Is an expression of living."

Toys faded and worn
Birth of joy reborn.

Sleeeeep
Why don't you come?
Why do you hide from me?
Am I to pursue
Another source of energy?

precarious journey
frightening
vulnerable
wonder-full

only the fool, the clown, risks
bewilderment by nocturnal light
silent rays
changing
penetrating
exposing
dissolving

How:

to compose
a sculpture of meaning
from life's constant
diversification,

to gather with devotion
jagged fragments
connected and disconnected
for careful observation,

to freeze insight
into a shimmering crystal?

High wire of life

                                I dance
                                facing

Forces unknown
Hazardous . . . . my journey
From rented home.

Like an eagle soaring

                                I risk
                                facing

Forces unknown
Dancing . . . . my myth
Creating my stone.

Like and eagle soaring

                                I dare
                                facing

Forces unknown
Captured by the lunar . . . . power
Of the philosopher's stone.

Projected glory becomes only a story;   ashes of self deceit. Presumptuous on-lookers stand in awe as the Emperor still walks clothed in nakedness, raw.

Who sees or saw?

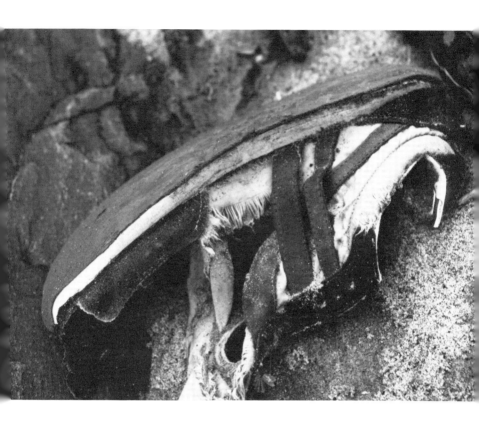

Heel   worn-down
Toe worn   through
Sole   parched
Tongue   tied

A weeping remnant
*   discarded*
Lingers   on the
Sand-bar of time.

Cast off!

Do not question. It is rude.
Remember, keep your place.
And when not in agreement
House a mask about your face.

　　　am I really to deter
　　　full consciousness of my "seeing,"
　　　can I not give honor
　　　to the vision of my "being."

　　　dare we not remember
　　　the breath of yester-year,
　　　wo/man trailed karma blindly,
　　　buried prophetic fear?

Shocking!　　　Tragic Behavior!
We speak with a righteous voice,
However, this moment,　　　to-day,
Do we carve on stone our inner choice?

A memory, retentive and secure
Stretched onto paper walls of time
Bleeds past into present
As future sculpts her own design.

A biting wind whips frustration over naked sea. Dark waves lash fiercely, uncontrollably, upon mother rock.

A small, stunned presence stands, contemplating the ocean's bottomless depth. She wrestles desperately trying to calm her own inner-churning sea, seeking that longed-for treasure hidden in the womb of darkness.

Day is ending.

a searching hand reaches
and pulls from your earth
a sticky glob of clay

centered
on the ever-turning
wheel of timelessness
a space is spun

form surrounds nothing

out of nothingness
an empty vessel
becomes a cup of
love.

DRAMA

To be as the "other" is
*   Youth   that dies*
To feel as the other feels
*   Splendor   of sunrise*
To know as the other knows
*   Problems unresolved*
To live as the other lives
*   Aware   involved*

Faded now the future path,
Buried at sea, life's long dreamt plan.

Walking on shifting, windswept shore,
Loneliness grips this a-lone man.

How does one extend beyond,
Discover knowns — unknowns hold?

In these sleepless hours of night
I find it hard to be so bold.

Youth's body stirs to light of day
Humming tunes of an old refrain,

Passionately wipes life's tarnished mirror,
Seeking desperately a soul to retain.

Aged body now longing with need
Descends twisted staircase once more,

As life and death holding hands
Wait quietly at revolving door.

How does one extend beyond,
Discover knowns' unknown thread?

My psyche willfully breathes
                (these sleepless nights)
Breath — of the awakened dead.

her ringless hand
ring streaked
carries
a promise(d) past
takes rise
feverishly
to paint
pastured clouds
wind-driven
that do not last
squinting skyward
beseeching eyes
perceive
and, her ringless hand
ring streaked
captures
the divergent light
of lifelong
shadows cast

THE RING

"Space
  between two circles
    having the same center"
Once dared we this sacred space to enter?

Edged yearly, new rings formed
  soft-winged winds abated storm.
Sturdy oak branches 'round us hung
  church bells pealed, future sung.
"A mighty sea ringing all the earth"
  protected womb's wondrous birth.

Long linked by wedded bond
  the ring — splits open,
Only echoes remain
  of Substance once lived and spoken.

Weeds grow tall
  choking untilled land
Erring footsteps
  mark seaside's hallowed sand.
How little we,
  the unawakened, understand.

"Space
  between two circles
    having the same center."
Once dared we this sacred space to enter?

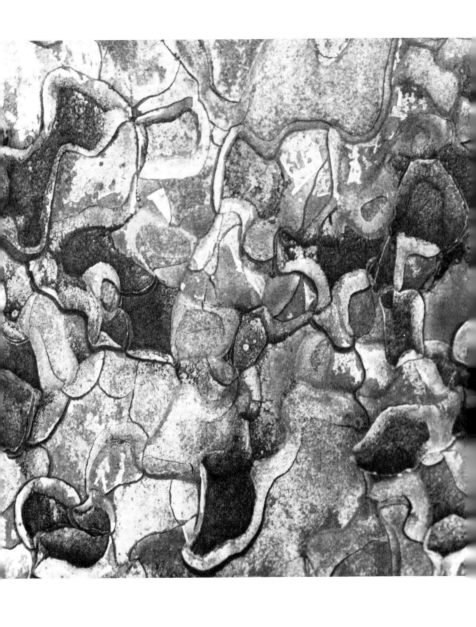

Shadow

    come
      sit by
   my side

Diversity travels both far and wide

Embraced by affection
     and salty tear
Within my shelled oyster
    a pearl appears

What truth lies not hidden
    blackened, unclear

Denying roots of a wounded being
We abort our moment of creative seeing.

We dream
We work
　　　with confined strength and determination
We unite
Possess
　　　with due consideration
We believe
Recline
　　　in silent meditation
We weave
Create
　　　our tapestry of hallucination
And forget
Nature's dying thread
Follows consecration.

Tears break
Death's desolate
Stilled sound.
Where is home
To be found?
Where?

Once more
  rejection clutches at self's emotional gut
  clamping off life with jaws of armored steel.

What   *that chokes,*
  as mirror   *bolts the door*
  am I fearfully   *to a natural rite*
  revealing,   *of healing?*

Nothing can I hold
                    or own
                    or ask.
Free the transcendent gift
Beneath an armored mask.

A flaming band of fire
a living torch
encircles my ego

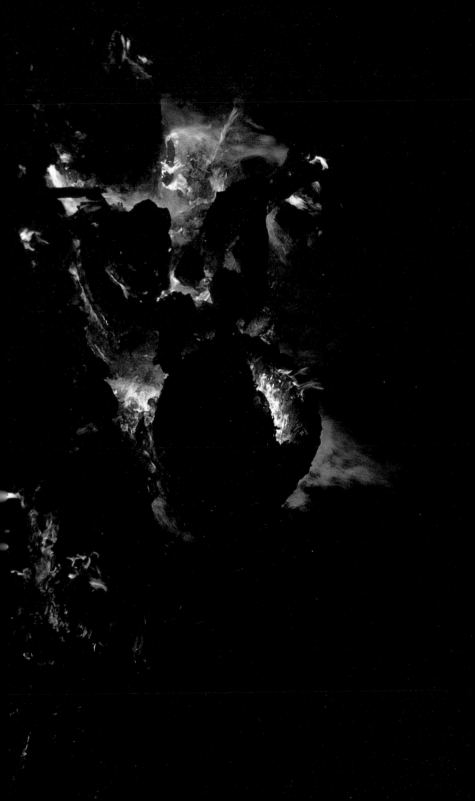

ALCHEMIST'S
FLASK

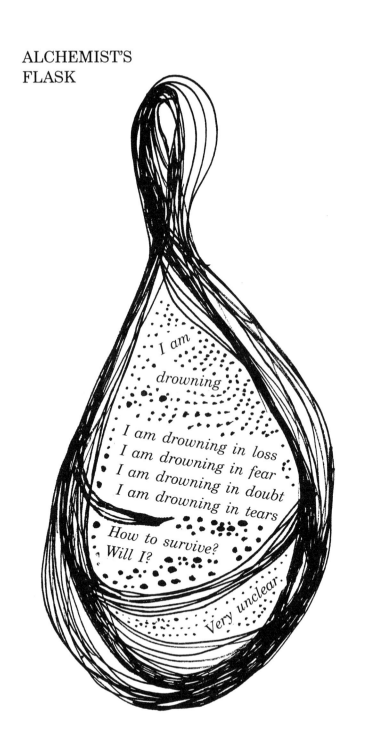

I am

drowning

I am drowning in loss
I am drowning in fear
I am drowning in doubt
I am drowning in tears

How to survive?
Will I?

Very unclear

What garment is this the spirit wears
As vessel powerless stands in despair,
Threatened before life's human abyss,
Dulled with horror of meaninglessness?

What garment is this the spirit wears
As she integrates failure into human fare,
Soul thrust into chaos against consent
Knowing drowns, truth becomes bent?

What garment is this the spirit wears
Demanding trust, a tension to bear?
Clay vessels center, wholeness breaks through,
Failures rejected are fashioned anew.

What garment is this the spirit wears
Instilling in hearts compassion to care,
Embracing the stranger, need of wo/man
Turning   each to the other,   gift of "I AM?"

What garment is this the spirit wears
As she summons soul to risk and to dare?
This hour! This space! Her being there-in
Peace,   only peace if contained within.

EGO LOSS

What did I lose
That I did not have.
*   What I thought I had?*

I,   who am I?
One preposterous lie
*   with what I think I have?*

Are we not born to die,
To lose the I?
*   So why do I cry?*

Because I think
It is I,   I
*   who propels self to fly?*

To live,   to have,
The ego must die.

O blind foolish eye,
Cease to cry.

To conquer death
Is to die.

Why will I never learn?
Why?

SOLO

Void
   dry as sun-bleached bone
      stilled upon sand's timeless bar

Silent
   wounded and lost
      buried within earth's mortal scar

Blessed
   inflamed soul
      transformed by night's ushering star.

DARK CORNERS

Shifting winds disperse earth-born mist,
(Invitation to exist)
Yet, I resist dark corners.

New seeds hide in shell of old,
(Fertile story often told)
Yet, I resist dark corners.

Inner journey, inner quest
(How else can blossom be my quest?)
Yet, I resist dark corners.

Detach the I, release resist
(Invitation to exist)
Passage through dark corners.

Opposing waves of undulation.

Swelling tides of contemplation.
Mirror-like pools of transformation.

TOOL MAKING

While walking
a rocky shore,
curious hands
selected
at random
two round stones
*   then*
seated beside
moving waters
*   spontaneously*
hammered
together
raw matter.
...breaking open
fragments scattered
and lo,
before me
lay tools of yesteryear
sharply formed
without notion of design.

Mind to select, direct, define.

RELATIONSHIP

You are the interior and exterior —
You are the restricted; the all encompassing
You are the strength and weakness
>   *Formed, yet you remain unformed*

You are light, and you are winter's darkness
You are servant and king, the created and
>   *Creator*
>   *Observer and observed, the beholder*
>   *and beheld*
You are the one and many
You are reality polarized —
You are truth polarized —
Be it personal or universal —
It is for us to synthesize.

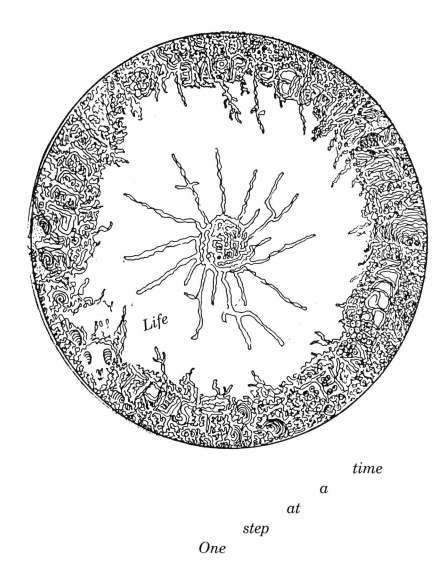

Life

time

a

at

step

One

Like the hill   *I daily climb*

Turning
Facing the sun
            gathering energy
For her continued run.

Beach   of tinted sand
I could linger all day

Drift   with your ocean
Gather moods on display

Caress each found pebble
Smooth next to my cheek

As touch evokes memory
Lost / Alive I yet seek

Coarse grains of uncertainty
Childlike I sift

Cross of contradiction
From the shifting sandbank I lift

"Learn His Source"
Tarry not too long.
Within, within Her
births love's sought song.

Unexpected mercy!

Unexpected gift!

Let pass
our tempo of yesterday,
a measure
now out of reach.

Only thought
of timeless presence
can penetrate
my contemplative beach.

A man-made fence,
    grey with age
    tilts forward.

    Silver grey mist from near ocean
    sweeps through time-ridden
    worm-eaten supports.

A sagging gate rests at an angle
    in grass long dead.

Pine trees protrude into fall's overcast sky,
    branches stark
    with decaying dreams
    of ages past.

Dreams strong and noble corralled by young hope.

    Today we silently watch yesterday's rented pas-
ture
    return to her original seed,

        unplanned and unequal this beauty
        escorted by tired fences
        and sagging gates open and grey.

    Is there any other way?

Bound in garments of worldly time
    mortal minds dance
      without fear
        into the lion's impassioned mouth

    Tragedy illuminates!

To silent ash the sharp silhouette
    of struggle falls
    Search stills in blinding
      light

Trembling
    one awakens to the sacred note
      of oaten flute
    breathing an ever prevailing
              concordance
    of the universe

'Tis a dark, sultry night.
Dawn has not yet broken.
Black people (many)
filled with repressed energy
link arms,
turn
and walk forward
creating
a solid moving wall.

They sing!
They wail!
Heads and bodies roll and weave
as they try
to break that constricting chain

which enslaves,
and wounds
and jangles
audibly within grounded ear.

In the moon-light
tears and sweat
mingle
forming
a glistening mass
of soft, pearl-like fish eggs
swirling at sea.

I now become one of them —

I stumble,
struggling
to drag the heavy metal
that encircles,
demeans
my very being.

I open
my thick, bleeding lips
to join in song.
This power-full
prayer-full petition
awakens me —

frees me.

How many forms do I possess,
Or am I possessed by, in number?

upstairs —

— downstairs

anima(l) prowls

Bridging east and west as I slumber.

Poetical images interweave,
supplanting logic with an elixir of awe
mortal wounds bid psyche to birth.
Soul-making, a primal intrinsic law.

Water flowing
Water still
Water rushing
Water mill

Water gate
Water shed
Water pail
Water fed

Water surging
Water swift
Water living
Water gift

Water golden
Water clear
Water healing
Water tear

Water woman
Water man
Water babbling
Water can

Water drip
Water drop
Water plug
Water stop

How can I with pen confine
Your swirling currents in one short line?

A leaf
One lone leaf   drifts — earth bound
Embraced by   season's divine reality, yesterday's
Silent death   becomes tomorrow's radiant birth

One of crimson glory.

Just yesterday
small hand in mine
first word
you formed to talk

Just yesterday
small hand in mine
I watched
you learn to walk

Just yesterday
small hand in mine
you waved
good-bye to play

Just yesterday
small hand in mine
so soon
became today.

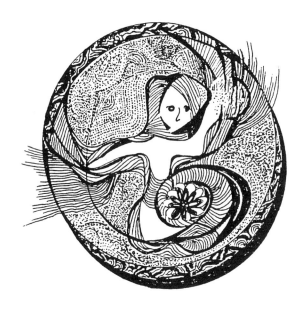

The forest beckons a small child,
   pensive and lonely
      she runs into shadowed solitude
     as pulsating heart
        beats against imprisoned walls

Bounding footsteps carry her troubled soul
    into its very center,
     searching eyes climb
      tall, friendly trees
            up

       up

  up
into the highest of heights,
    into a world
      of cloudless dreams.

A stream nearby whispers a spirit of welcome

Her healing waters tumble tenderly
over naked rock
purifying and sculpting
as she touches.

Deep-reaching is the journey
returning
to one's primal source.

Next to the cave-like base
of an old gnarled redwood
ferns and soft needles
caress the child's
now motionless body.

Here —
concealed in darkness
the hidden treasure unfolds
as mother earth enfolds and transforms
this tiny, young seed
into
a flowering tree of knowledge.

hidden seed —
                    fortunes untold
there you lie —
                    damp and cold

waiting
                    waiting
                              waiting
waiting
                    waiting
                              waiting

waiting

                              waiting

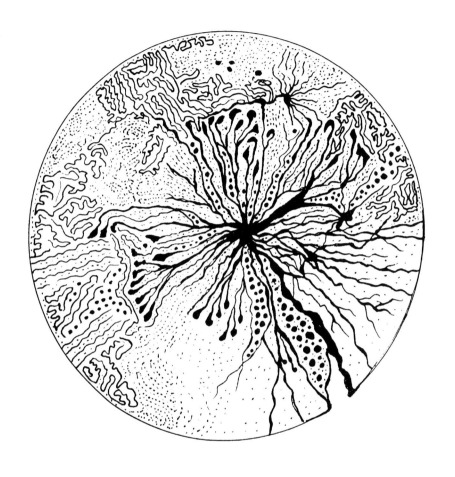

from a cracked boulder you emerge
never to thirst
as root and life's spring converge

I,   a seed
And the plan
To become what I can
To respond
To expand
To bend to the touch
Of the potter's hand.

TAPESTRY

Unless we filter
　　　　what we assume

Question
　　　　what we believe

Eyes will betray
　　　　what we perceive

Unknown
　　　　that distorted truth
　　　　we help weave —— —

A DREAM

Frustrated with power and weakness,
                    life's ambitious game.
I yearn to step outside of time
Beyond the grip of name.

Here, rapid pulse is slowed to rest,
Space stilled in shape-less form;
And moments of shattered madness
collect, await, transform.

Light strikes dream's polished prism,
Earth's heightened spectrum seen
As fragments shimmer in wholeness
And feed the miracle of being.

IN AWE

We stand
> *before sea's vastness*
Pondering,
Waiting,
> *as a canvas*
> *awaits the framed stroke*
> *of an artist's hand.*

Slowly,
> *from unbound space*
> *a veil of mist appears,*
> *wrapping all visibility*
> *in a sheath of invisibility.*

Lost —
> *in this "cloud of unknowing"*
We discover
> *the hidden self.*

QUINTA ESSENTIA

A simple pot
        formed of clay
Porous
        breathing breath of day
Protector
        of earth's pregnant seed
Container
        for   all   growing need
Wellspring
        of void's hallowed space
Ancient symbol
        of woman's inner grace.

O vessel fragile   vessel strong

Infuse my being
        with your sacred note
        with your cosmic song.

INTUITION?

Someone is touching my hand.
Have I not felt this touch before?
Uncanny penetration
Acutely affects my inner core.

Hope
  are you granting formation
  of an unwritten score;
  visibility to an invisible shore?

ADVERSITY

Is there any pattern in our tapestry
of daily living
more difficult to weave:
acting spontaneously with trust?

To receive all strands that enter
      as gift,
      as lesson,
      as texture,
      as color.

Yes, even to accept those unacceptable
strands one cannot accept.

Oh, to be so adept.

Spirit - Breath

Fear penetrates wounded heart,
Valves sputter, stutter, stop and start
Darkness laces every vein.
Life's woven strand ... becomes a chain!

O wind, merciful, shifting wind,
Will you ever breathe Hope
Into my valley again?

And what is this Hope
you seek to retain;
Yesterday's moorings - broken and strained?

Let go"... Let go"...
Self's constant refrain
Walk into .... dance thro
the purging flame
Depths fire and holy embers
Burn not the same
tho each etch'd with transform
thee Creator's name

dgc

SPIRIT BREATH

Fear penetrates wounded heart.
Valves sputter, stutter, stop, start.
Darkness laces every vein,
Life's woven strand becomes a chain.

> *O wind, merciful, shifting wind,*
> *Will you ever breathe Hope*
> *Into my valley again?*

> *And what is this Hope*
> *You seek to retain,*
> *yesterday's mooring, broken and strained?*

Let go!   Let go!
Self's constant refrain.
Walk into   dance through
My burning flame.
Earth's fire and Holy embers
Are not the same,
Though each etch with transforming light
The Creator's name.

Am I   attempting
     to breathe the breath of false illusion again,
to rediscover
     that which does not transform, denies "to be?"

Unbroken
 is the chain of revelation that life
 exhibits.
Bewildered
 one stands wrapped in unsolved mystery.
Bound
 by flesh and speculation, we run to escape
 her iron weight of inflicting pain,
 her dark windings of light to logical brain.
Impulsively
 we resist change's link of hidden salvation,
Blindly
 forget life's labyrinth holds procreation.

Like the 'wild ox' tamed
 in ancient civilization
Must we too
 learn to taste
   feel
   live
Carry *life's paradox and its ramification?*

Hollow . . . . is the tree of death
Ever shifting . . . . . . wind's spiritual
invisible breath

CHANGE

Locked in time's landscape I stood
capturing fields of childhood

> *bachelor buttons, purple vetch,*
> *butterflies I raced to catch*

> *dandelions   yellow-bright,*
> *fluffy pappus taking flight*

> *scented clover, purple-green*
> *scouring rush, tallest seen*

> *red-brown trillium all a-bloom,*
> *icicles gleaming, hung from flume.*

Lost Creek's winding, ceaseless talk,
soaring birds in endless flock

> *wind-spun clouds swept summer sky,*
> *image enamored youthful eye*

Abandoned now the old mill fades,
gone the trees that gave cool shade.
A bunk-house leans next silent hill,
dry weeds hang from sagging sill.

> *Boundless memories as I stand*
> *watching   change   take my hand.*

THE SEEDLING

Answering unknown's known, gnawing need.

When I was but a little child, my father's careful hands planted, in sifted soil, a young larch. Spur-like branches soon spread, bearing tufts of light green needles from her open crowns. I watched in wonder at the bright red cones turning to a darker red. Then, when ripe, they became a chestnut brown, still clinging to the deciduous tree.

Now, failing, molding branches droop, as shoulders stoop. And, a child, no longer a child, carefully transplants a memory.

McKENZIE RIVER

Deep within the shadowed forest of birth,
clay feet carry   self   to river's
        soft
                green
                        moss-laden banks.

Walking through ancient corridors
mind and soul contemplate,
        and awaken thought
                etched upon inner walls
                of consciousness.

Although fragmented,
this porous earthen vessel
        contains   Self,
                that she might reveal
                        wisdom hidden in the waters

                of eternity.

THE MASTER POTTER

...and her skilled hands responded
With the most intricate of feeling,
As she turned earth's raw lump of clay.

With inner strength and vision,
Form, volume and line   quickened
In a balanced and functional way.

"Throwing is discovery of self,"
Liberation of mind and soul,
She counseled firmly   day after day.

And now, the turning wheel rests
Stilled   by time.
But the 'good pot' endures,
Her invisible substance   divine.

Silent witness:
The potter's favorite, wild rose vine.

Her being, like time's undulating breath
  carries segments joyful
  transports segments deep
    is hesitant, as passages wind
      narrow and steep.

Implicit trust in changing seasons
Her yearning soul spins to keep.

Removing
Burning
Filtering
  always that which was there.

Replacing
Renewing
Discovering
  with sustaining fresh air.

Between the breath
  beyond
    behind
Rests the stilled fullness
  she seeks to find

    Pearl of cosmic time.

O boundless blue mid-summer sky

You tease my child to an ecstatic high

As bright-winged bird I sing and fly

As kindred tree I sway

With fallen leaf I spin and glide

And drop my feet of clay

FINAL FALL

O man
by what will do we tear apart
the self from rooted season,
And in pride
of spoken language
choose to name it reason?
Mind scans
a vast and awesome power
sun's elements now perceived
Cosmic rhythm
inherent in its structure
also known, believed.
Yet lock
we do, a tiny sun
uncontrolled in greedy hand
To blast
to ash, in name of reason
the living art of man.
O man
by what will do we tear apart
the self from rooted season,
And in pride
of spoken language
name this slaughter reason?

MUSIC OF THE SPHERES

we are but strings
a cosmic instrument
pulsating
oscillating
vibrating
embracing
life's present moment
participating
in a greater symphony

FEMININE PRINCIPLE

Sophia
Supreme Goddess
Resplendent One

Compassionate
Merciful
Bearer of Son

Corn Maiden
Weaver, weaving
Threads to be sung

Disturbing
Unpredictable
"Stirring up" (Jung)

Persistent
Courageous
Concealed in dung

Essential chaos
From which
All existence comes

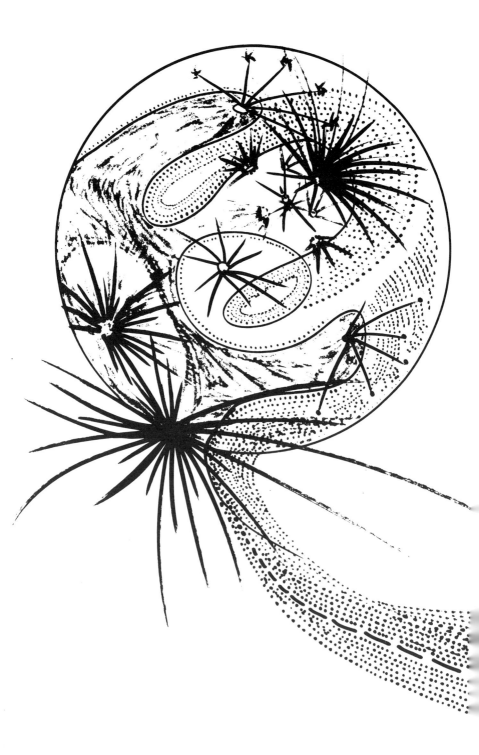

SURPRISE

. . . upon the path
a dragon stalked
and cornered
its wounded prey,
blossoms drooped,
grasses wept,
dark night
swallowed
light of day.
...as her
wing-like claws
and breath of fire
burst into
showering flame,
across the sky
a million stars
spelled in gold
my name.

Sun-lit dew drop
 on life's wire you cling
 tenacious
  sparkling
  bright

Becoming
 the river
 the sea
  a diamond
  for me
Being this moment

   Eternity.

Words share
Words scare

Words inquire
Words inspire

Words sort
Words distort

Words hope
Words cope

Words reject
Words connect

Words express
Words bless

Words measure
Words treasure

Words tame
Words name

Words review
Words renew

Word Became

tempest of the sea
  crashes
  lashes
  smashes
  stubborn walls of security

CREATIVE EVENT

Indeed, the river of living rushes,
and alas! Chaotically flushes
Though each tone be clear and single,
notes collide, transform and mingle.

In that transient space
        silent
        and
        full of sound,
A cosmic star
        afar —
        births
        within
Soul's earthen jar.

FINAL CUT TO FREEDOM

A photo stands upon a carved shelf. Its corners faded and worn. I cannot remember when it was not there. As a child these two solemn faces, man and woman, side by side, looked down upon me with unquestionable knowledge. Today, I see an unbridled energy and a determination only known to immigrants from the old country.

And now — this moment, I gaze at an elderly, frail, ninety-four year old woman. She is sitting in a wheelchair, frustrated, crying and tugging at a white strap that binds her to an unwanted limitation. Her sunken eyes hold unmistakably the same fire and determination as those in the old photo. How well I remember! And not always, I must confess, with the most pleasant recall. Mother's dream, to be executed, called for threads of woven perfection.

She trembles with anger as her fingers can no longer untangle life's entanglements. Do we ever cease struggling with umbilical cords that bind and confine?

> *From birth on*
> *we are cut free*
> *to be tied*
> *over and over and over.*
> *Ever ongoing,*
> *this uroboric process.*

Beneath her worn and wrinkled face, I see a little girl weeping, admonished by a stern parent for venturing too far from the protective hand. What are we protecting?

I see, too, this moment, my daughters and sons gazing at me with like thoughts, as I struggle with the next given umbilical cord that ties and binds. What precious gift, that mind diminishes the memory of time, as self makes her passage. What a blessing, and indeed cause for celebration, that final cut — to freedom.

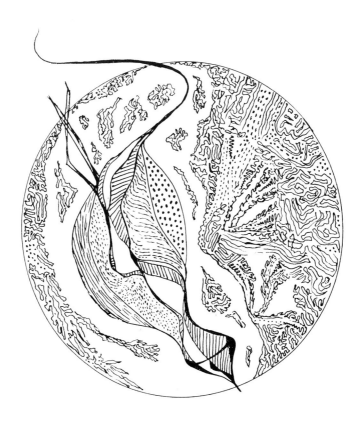

stillness
virtue
returning
    to source
yielding
accepting
nature's
shaping
    course
silent
manifestation
primordial
    force

I watch
  fall's barren, inter-lacing branches
  write calligraphy across cloudless sky

  russet leaves blanket waiting earth
  drifting from parent with peaceful sigh

I see
  bending weeds drop deathless seeds
  profusely onto sleepy ground

I hear
  scented breeze quietly murmur
  her healing, musical sound

I feel
  nestled in grass, a ruby chalice
  last radiant blossom of her kind

  time drawing to a timeless halt, as
  deep thought retreats from a curious mind

Grateful
  for this reflective moment
  for season's gift of seeing

  as God reveals   breathes Self
  into harmony of all created being.